SPEECHES

DELIVERED

AT A DINNER GIVEN TO THE

HON. DANIEL WEBSTER

BY THE

REFORM CONVENTION OF MARYLAND,

AT ANNAPOLIS, TUESDAY, MARCH 25, 1851.

WASHINGTON:
GIDEON & CO., PRINTERS.
1851.

SPEECHES

DELIVERED

AT A DINNER GIVEN TO THE

HON. DANIEL WEBSTER

BY THE

REFORM CONVENTION OF MARYLAND,

AT ANNAPOLIS, TUESDAY, MARCH 25, 1851.

WASHINGTON:
GIDEON & CO., PRINTERS.
1851.

SPEECHES.

Gov. SPRIGG offered the following toast, which was received with prolonged applause:

"DANIEL WEBSTER—Maryland shows her attachment to the Union by honoring its ablest defender."

After the applause had subsided, MR. WEBSTER rose and addressed the gentlemen of the convention, as follows:

MR. PRESIDENT AND GENTLEMEN: I beg leave to assure you that I esteem most highly this testimony of respect. I find myself in the political capital of the loyal, Union State of Maryland; I find myself at a table at which many of the most distinguished men of that State, of all parties and descriptions of politics, are assembled. And it is on that account that I regard this as a particular and striking mark of respect and honor to myself. But, gentlemen, I am nothing; it is the cause that is every thing. You are pleased to honor me only because I support, so far as my ability will allow, that cause which is dear to us all, and dear to all good men in the country. It is the cause of the Union. It is the cause of the preservation of the States. It is the cause upon which depends the maintenance of all those political associations and principles which have made the United States what they now are.

It is not for me to argue the value of the Union in this company. I came here rather to be refreshed and edified by what I have heard of the proceedings of this Convention already, upon that subject. Its resolutions of the 10th of December are to me an expression so powerful, so authentic, and so conclusive of the judgment of Maryland, that I read them at first, and have read them since, and read them now, with undiminished delight. Why, gentlemen, I should no more think of arguing the question of the importance of the Union in this assembly, than I should think of going back to argue the propriety of the Declaration of Independence, or to argue the expediency and the glory of having adopted the Constitution under which we live, or of arguing the general utility and honor and renown of Washington's administration. Who doubts all these things here? I am sure not one. I come, then, gentlemen, as a learner, not as a teacher; I come to partake of the sentiments that fill all your hearts; I come to be edified and instructed by those noble and patriotic expositions which have been made in this Convention, formed, as I have said, of distinguished men of all parties, coming together with earnest convictions, and affirming their opinions in favor of the Union, and whatsoever tends to strengthen that Union, by a unanimity which cannot fail to be regarded. Allow me to say, gentlemen, that your resolutions of the 10th of December will reach to the extreme North, the extreme South, and the extreme West, and every body will say that, amidst all the vagaries which may prevail elsewhere, the respectable, and eminent, and distinguished State, the central State of Maryland, is union to the backbone, and thoroughly. [Applause.]

There are associations, there are recollections, which naturally influence the minds of men. I have passed around, to-day, among scenes which were visited in old times by Washington. I have been in the room where he performed that crowning act of his military life, the resignation of his commission. I remember that he said on that occasion, "having finished the work assigned me, I now claim the indulgence of retiring from the service of my country." Gentlemen, Washington, with all his sagacity, did not comprehend his own destiny. He did not see the long track of influences which were to follow his revolutionary character. Nay, nor when, many years afterwards, he retired from the civil administration of the country, did he then cease to exercise an influence on the public concerns and sentiments of his country. And he never will cease. He said, "having finished the work assigned me, I retire from public service." He has never yet performed the work assigned him, and he never will, until the end of time; because, gentlemen, that great and glorious work still subsists, and is going on; he is still upholding, by his precepts, his exhortations, and his example, the importance and the value of this Union of the States. [Applause.] In that respect he works now, and will work ever, so long as his memory shall not be effaced from the records of mankind. I think I hear him say to-day, in the language which he expressed when he sent the present Constitution of the United States to Congress, "in all our deliberations we have kept steadily in view that which appeared to us the greatest interest of every true American, the consolidation of our Union, in which is involved our prosperity, felicity, safety, perhaps our national existence." I hear him say that to-day, and I hear him say further to-day, in the words of his Farewell Address, "indignantly frown upon the first dawning of every attempt to alienate any portion of our country from the rest, or to enfeeble the sacred ties which now link together the various parts." Every exhortation, every admonition, every sentiment that proceeded from him, rings in these times constantly in my ears. Nay, I think I hear him say now, in the abodes of the blessed, that, if it were permitted to him, to revisit the earth, and be re-clothed with the bones and the flesh which are mouldering at Mount Vernon, he would appear to his countrymen as when he stood at the head of their armies, or as he appeared to the country in the course of his most glorious administration of this Government, and conjure and adjure them, by every consideration that ought to have weight with men, "Hold on fast by that Constitution which is the only security for the liberty which cost me and my associates seven years of war, of fire, and of blood." [Applause.]

Gentlemen, forgive me; when I think in these times that there are so many that are apparently disposed to undervalue the maxims, and the character, and the exhortations of Washington, I confess I find myself borne away, often beyond the power of self-restraint; I fear sometimes beyond the limits of propriety. Our country consists in its elements of liberty; in its institutions of constitutional law; and, blessed be God, our country, America, consists next in the great example of those who have gone before us, and have left that example for our imitation and encouragement. We are not Americans if we resist the examples of our predecessors, any more than if we trample upon the Constitution, the work of their hands. If we have real American hearts in our bosoms, every thing they said, and every thing they did, to honor and ennoble their country, impresses us with sentiments of profound respect and regard.

Gentlemen, will you allow me to interrupt the course of my remarks by proposing to you, out of the fulness of my heart, *"The glorious and immortal memory of George Washington!"* [This toast was drank standing.]

Mr. Webster resumed. Mr. President and gentlemen: In the lapse of years, and in the rising of one generation after another, it may very possibly happen, and we are sure that it does happen, and has happened, that the exact principles of the Union of these States are not always properly understood. It may not be amiss, therefore—though I do not propose to entertain this company by discourse upon common-places—it may not be amiss, to recur, now, to what I conceive to be the original principle upon which these colonies were united, the objects for which they were united, and the limitations upon these objects. These thirteen colonies, all of English origin, were settled on this continent at different times, and under different circumstances. They had differences of religious opinions; they established differences of local law and administration; they were, some of them, quite remote from one another, but they were all subject to the crown of England. And when, in the course of events, they all thought, and thought truly, they had just cause of complaint against the tyranny of England, their object was to unite in a common cause against a common enemy. How unite? For what purposes unite? For what ends unite? Why, it never entered into their conceptions that they were to consolidate themselves into one integral government; that they were to cease to be Virginia, Maryland, Massachusetts, and Carolina. Not at all. But they were to unite for those great purposes which should enable them to make a stand against the injustice of the English Government. They were to unite for common defence, and the general welfare. They were to come to an agreement upon things necessary for that purpose, and nothing else. The objects of common defence, and the general welfare, and afterwards the objects connected with commerce and revenue, which were important to all, were all they adopted as principles and objects of union and association. Nothing beyond that.

As I have said, they had differences of religious opinions. Maryland, your Maryland, was settled as a Catholic country, always tolerant, always liberal, persecuting nobody. Virginia was rather inclined to the religious notions of the Episcopal Church of England. The people of the North were not only Protestants but Dissenters. They were of the school of Cromwell and Sir Henry Vane. But what of that? When all these colonies came together for the general purpose of defence against a common enemy, what did they do? Did they seek to merge, and confound, and consolidate all these States into one great community? No such thing. They meant to unite upon those objects which were necessary for the common defence; and they meant to leave every thing else in the control of the States, to do just as they thought proper. That was a day of liberality and of justice. It was a day in which religious opinions produced no effect upon the general sentiments of the country in regard to the association of all the States for common objects. Why, sir, did any body at the North, did any Protestant descending from ancestors inheriting the principles of Cromwell, or of Harry Vane, whoever he was, feel any less confidence in the integrity and entire patriotism of Charles Carroll, because he was a Catholic? Not at all. Nor did Maryland hesitate to accord the meed of patriotism, whenever it was due, to the Adamses, to Alexander Hamilton, to Rufus King, or whoever else belonged to the North, because they were of different sentiments in religion. Their association was political. It was founded upon general policy and union; a sort of confederacy, at that time, to resist the common enemy, and to do whatever was necessary for the common good. Gentlemen, I hope, for one, never to see this original idea departed from.

Now, we come to other propositions. There were differences of laws. The Southern States, without their own fault, by a course of events for which they were not responsible, had slavery established amongst them

Did not all the States know that? Did not they deal with them upon that basis? Did not they recognise that state of things? Entirely; entirely. That was a matter of local legislation, of State right and State administration, with which the North at that time had not the slightest inclination to interfere in any respect whatever; and they ought not to have had, because it was one of those things that did not enter into the general scope of that political association which the colonies meant to establish.

Gentlemen, I concur in the sentiments, expressed by you all; and, thank God, they were expressed by you all in the resolutions passed here on the 10th of December. You say that "the Constitution of the United States has accomplished all the objects, civil and political, which the most sanguine of its framers and friends anticipated, and that the affections of the people of Maryland are justly riveted to its principles by the memory of the characters of the wise and good men who formed it, as well as by the blessings they liberally bestow throughout the world." That is my sentiment. My heart is in it. [Applause.] Altogether, I live and breathe, I walk and sleep—I had almost said, I pray to God daily, in the very sentiment of that resolution. Then you go on to assert a sentiment equally just. You say that a proper appreciation of those blessings would lead every State in the Union to adopt all such measures as may from time to time be necessary to give complete and full effect to any provision in the Constitution, or the laws pursuant thereto, intended for the protection of any part of this great common country. True; every word true. And allow me to say, that any State, North or South, which departs an iota from the sentiment of that resolution, is disloyal to this Union. [Great applause.]

Further, so far as any act of that sort has been committed, such a State has no portion of my regard. I do not sympathize with it. I rebuke it wherever I speak, and on all occasions where it is proper for me to express my sentiments. If there are States, and I am afraid there are, which have sought, by ingenious contrivances of State legislation, by roundabout and crooked courses of policy, to thwart the just operation and fulfilment of the laws of Congress passed to carry into effect the compacts of the Constitution, that State, so far, is entitled to no regard from me.

At the North, there have been certainly some intimations in certain States of such a policy.

At the South, another danger seems to have arisen; and it is a subject of very serious lamentation to me. It would seem that there is a disposition in some quarters to secede from the Union of these States. "Secede!" a word of ominous import. Secede from what? Secede from this Government, which has carried the country to such a pitch of glory in sixty or seventy years? To secede from all the honor and renown which it has accomplished? And to secede where? Whenever there is *a terminus a quo* there is *a terminus ad quem.* Where are they going? [Applause.] Whoever entertains such sentiments I regard with a spirit of commiseration. I think it is a malady of the mind. I think that their feelings have become entirely diseased. I think that they know not what they do. And yet, gentlemen, I do not think it the part of prudence to criminate, or to taunt, or to provoke. Leave them to their own consideration. Let them dwell on secession many days and inwardly digest it. [Laughter.] And, so far as I have any voice in the councils of the country, this meditation of theirs shall never be disturbed; not a breath shall ruffle their sensibility, until it comes to a point where something is done, which comes to an actual conflict with the Constitution and the laws. [Applause.]

It is painful when we reflect that a State so highly distinguished, so full of high spirits and cavaliers, a State which took such an active part in the Revolution, and which took such an active part also in the early administration of the Government, which has produced so many men who have honored the country, and honored themselves in the public service; it is painful, I say, and humiliating, to consider that their successors, the present generation, seem willing to forget all the glories of their country, and to take one stripe and one star and walk out of the Union with them. [Laughter.]

A returning sense of patriotism and propriety will check them. I do not know what might happen if there had been a more general spirit of disunion. But I cannot persuade myself that honest and honorable men, ingenuous men, young men who wish to live for glory, and renown, and character, will ever leave that Union which their fathers established, that Constitution which has made their State, like all the other States, what it is, when they come to sober moments of reflection.

I hope that while we maintain, as the State of Maryland has maintained, fixed and determined sentiments in favor of the Constitution, we shall hold no parley, and I hold no parley, with any body who would infract it in the slightest degree. While we maintain the necessity of establishing and sustaining those laws of adjustment which were passed by the last Congress, to settle the country; while we hold on to them with firmness and decision, I hope, nevertheless, we shall take a course not to provoke, or taunt, or insult those who feel a difference of sentiments. I hold the importance of maintaining those measures to be of the highest character and nature, every one of them, out and out, and through and through. [Applause.] I have no confidence in any body who seeks the support of those who wish to alter or modify these constitutional provisions. There they are. Many of these great measures are irrepealable. The settlement with Texas is as irrepealable as the admission of California. Other important objects of legislation, if not in themselves in the nature of grants, and therefore not so irrepealable, are just as important; and we are to hear no parleying upon it. We are to listen to no modifications or qualification endangering their security. They are passed in conformity with the requisitions of the Constitution; and they must be performed and abided by, in whatever event, and at whatever cost. [Applause.]

His Excellency the Governor of Maryland was pleased to allude to me as one who had run some risks among his own people for the good of the country. What should I have been good for, if I had not been willing to do it? [Applause.] I do not consider myself born to any great destiny, but born to one destiny, and that is, to uphold, with mind and heart and hand, the Constitution of this country. [Great applause.] If this prophecy fail, my attachment to the Constitution of the land will never fail, so long as I have breath. [Renewed applause.]

Now, gentlemen, allow me to say, that, in looking over the annals of your beautiful city of Annapolis, I find, what I should have expected to find, that when the definitive treaty of peace was proclaimed here in February, 1783, it was ordained to be a day of general thanksgiving. It was celebrated, and, according to the good fashions of Maryland, there was a dinner, and a ball. Among the toasts on that occasion, the first having taken notice of the great blessing of the restoration of peace, I find that the second was, "The United States—may their confederacy endure forever." [Applause.] That confederacy has been changed into a more beneficial form of government. It has become a Constitution better calculated to secure the rights of us all. But I echo the sentiment of Annapolis, and I say, in different words, though in the same sense, "*The Constitution of the United States—may it endure forever.*" [Great applause.]

The President offered *the second regular toast:*

"THE GOVERNOR OF MARYLAND."

Governor LOWE said:

MR. PRESIDENT AND GENTLEMEN: In responding to the compliment paid me, as the Executive of Maryland, in the sentiment which you have so kindly offered, and which has been so flatteringly received by this assemblage of distinguished friends, I should, under ordinary circumstances, confine my remarks to a simple expression of thanks and reciprocal esteem. But, sir, we meet here to-day upon no common occasion, and for no slight purpose. It is not that we may gather around the festive board for the pleasing interchange of wit, or the less spiritual indulgences of conviviality, that we are here to-day. Neither is it solely because we would honor the genius and the public services of your distinguished guest, that this company has assembled here, ably representing, as it does, the hospitality, the statesmanship, and the patriotism of Maryland. We are here to honor genius, and to bear testimony to eminent patriotism, surely; but we are here, in an especial manner, to approve and vindicate the laws of our native land, by honoring a man who has stood, and stands, as a champion, in the foremost ranks, battling against the enemies of the Constitution and the Union. We are here, too, to say to the people of this confederacy, and to the friends of human freedom every where, that Maryland, in heart and soul, in ancient memories, in present affections, and in future hopes, by every tie and by every sympathy, is, and ever will, with God's blessing, continue to be, a UNION STATE! And I here say, in the presence of the North, (*for the North is present!*) that Maryland can never be driven from the Union, so long as her continuance therein is compatible with the happiness and the honor of her people.

Maryland's southern heart is loyal to the Constitution and the laws of our common country; let only her southern rights be appreciated and respected. I have heard much, sir, of a "*higher law,*" a law above the laws of the land; a law of individual conscience, which assumes to instigate and canonize treason! Sir, when this Constitution, under the shadow of which the South has ever claimed sanctuary when her rights have been threatened, was first framed by the sacred hands of our fathers, there was, indeed, a "*higher law,*" which dwelt in the hearts of men, and the reflection of which, only, has been imparted to their works. Upon no written parchments, however excellent, could human language have transcribed the full soul of that law, as it breathed in the heart of Washington and the men of his generation.

It was the law of justice, of fraternity, of boundless self-abnegation, which led to the establishment of an unprecedented confederacy of States, upon a broad and liberal compromise of interests and opinions. Thank God, that "*higher law*" yet lives in our day!

Amidst the storm of passions, and encompassed by treason, it yet struggles on, with unquenchable flame, lighting the path of good men.

Sir, have we no evidence that we are not a degenerate race, unworthy of our sires? What was it but this "*higher law*" which interrupted the routine of parties, and swept away for the time old political land-marks, as the ocean wave effaces the tracks upon the beach—what was it, but this, I say, that made Webster and Cass shake hands, after a party antagonism of forty years! All honor to such men; such heroes, sir! For, are they not the genuine heroes? Tell me not, sir, of the hero of the battle-field. I would not depreciate his merit; yet, tell me what it is? Is it, that he has faced a thousand cannon, and looked composedly upon a sea of nodding plumes? From the beginning of the world, millions of men have done this, and millions may again do it before time drops the curtain of this world's drama. What of all that? It is courage, it is heroism, if you please; yet, sir, it is of the earth, earthy. Oh! there is a heroism of deeper signification and power; and which lies at the foundation of the most exalted human nature, and without possessing which, in more or less degree, no man can be truly great, in himself, or in his acts.

It is, sir, the heroism of a VIRTUOUS AND UNCONQUERABLE WILL, which the warring elements of nature cannot shake, nor human power move,

> Justum et tenacem propositi virum,
> Non civium ardor prava jubentium,
> Non vultus instantis tyranni,
> Mente quatit solida!

Can you fail to make the application? Have we not in our midst, this day, a bright illustration of the poet's noble estimate of moral heroism?

Within those lines are contained two tests, which have filled history with examples of greatness, but in far different proportions.

> Non vultus instantis tyranni!

What, sir, is the frown of one tyrant? Thousands have strung their courage to resistance against kings! Thousands have looked a monarch in the eye, even from the scaffold! There was often a conscious pride, which sustained, when his ordinary nature would have failed, the victim of imperial wrath.

> Non civium ardor prava jubentium!

That, sir, is the test, that the fiery ordeal, which searches the vitals of greatness, and tries its value! And comparatively few, indeed, when fully tried, have equalled the crisis. As public opinion, when sound and tolerant, is the conservative power of a free nation, so, when depraved and vindictive, it is the most formidable of tyrants. Who can fathom the depth of that courage, which makes an honest man stand up in his own community to rebuke injustice to its face? What self-complacency can we, Marylanders, gather from our open demonstrations of patriotic adhesion to the laws of the land, when here, in our honored State, no man dare whisper treason or disunion? Where the test of courage, when a

Maryland statesman proclaims the inviolability of the Compromise acts to a people who unitedly approve and support them? In patriotic Maryland, the only avenue to the popular heart is through loyalty to the Constitution and the laws! But, sir, in other sections of this Union it is, unfortunately, otherwise. Powerful factions exist, aye, and wield a fearful influence, whose avowed purpose it is to set at defiance the rights of the South in violation of solemn constitutional guaranties and legislative enactments, even should the vast fabric of this confederate Government crash around their unholy heads.

When I find a man, born in their midst, nurtured into a world-wide fame by their encouragement, bound to them by all earthly ties, standing up in the dignity of his mission as a leader of American destinies, and openly without fear, calmly without passion, and sternly without compromise, rebuking the folly or the crime of his own people, I cannot but exclaim with the great Roman bard—

Non civium ardor prava jubentium,
* * * * * * *
Mente quatit solida!

Yes, sir, the intellect of our distinguished guest, and his unconquerable resolve, are "*solid,*" like the granite hills of old New Hampshire, which gave him to his country and mankind!

Allow me, sir, to offer the following sentiment—

The "*higher law*" of patriots, which lifts them above the law of party, when the Constitution and the Union are in danger.

The following toast was then offered:

"The Senate of the United States: The rights of the State and the integrity of the Union have a sure protection in its wisdom and firmness."

Ex-Governor PRATT, at present a Senator of the United States, responded to this sentiment as follows:

The services of Mr. WEBSTER, to which you have referred, and which have been the immediate cause of your invitation to him, were services rendered to the *whole* country, and he is your guest at the capital of Maryland by the invitation (without distinction of party) of the Representatives of the People of Maryland, because *his* patriotism has not been limited by the State which he has represented, or by the section of country from which he comes. He is, Mr. President, properly here the guest of a Southern State, because the United States is *his country*—because the United States is *the country* to which he has declared *his* allegiance, and devoted all the energies of his vast intellect. I am pleased, too, Mr. President, that the invitation which gives us the pleasure of this meeting, should have emanated as it has, irrespective of party; for, sir, if we may now congratulate ourselves upon the safety of our country, we should ever remember that the threatened danger has been arrested by no party, or party men, but by the united efforts of those of the Democratic and Whig parties of the country who have been most trusted and honored by each.

If, sir, a citizen of Annapolis may be permitted to say so, I think the place has been appropriately selected for this meeting. Annapolis, now the capital of the State of Maryland, was, prior to the Revolution, not only the capital of the then province of Maryland, but socially, and in point of political influence, was, as your distinguished guest has intimated, the capital of all the British North American provinces. Mr. Webster has referred to some of the historical reminiscences attached to the place, and I beg leave, sir, to refer to others which I have heard here spoken of, and which I had hoped he would have also referred to. Here, sir, at Annapolis, was held the first Council, composed of delegates from several of the then British provinces, to deliberate and decide upon the necessity of resistance to the encroachments of the Crown. Here, also, if I am correctly informed, (and no one can more readily put me right than the distinguished gentleman before me,) was committed the first overt act of what was then called treason, by the open and forcible resistance of a statute of Parliament; and here, Mr. President, in the Senate chamber this day visited by your guest, occurred one of the most memorable and extraordinary events recorded in the history of the world, the surrender by Gen. Washington, to the civil authorities, of that sword with which he had achieved the independence of his country.

I have learned, Mr. President, in the past twelve months, a lesson which this meeting is well calculated to enforce. I have learned, sir, to rid myself of much, I hope of all, that political *party* asperity which I fear I have heretofore almost cherished as a duty. How, sir, could it be otherwise? I have followed the lead of men of the Democratic party, and stood side by side with them in support of the measures to which you, sir, have referred, and to which, in my judgment, you have correctly attributed the present existence of the Union. And here, Mr. President, I am surrounded by many, whose moral and social worth have been always appreciated by me, but with whom I have never acted politically, assembled together to do honor and to express respect for Daniel Webster. And, Mr. President, we may all well unite in paying this homage to such a man; for, sir, if there is a statesman in the United States who may be considered above party, and for whom all may express respect and admiration, that man is Daniel Webster. Sir, in all questions in which his country is involved, he knows no party. As he himself has said, he was born an American, he has lived an American, and he will die an American.

Permit me, Mr. President and gentlemen, to offer a sentiment, which I know will meet the approbation of your guest, and which I hope will also be favored by your approval. Gentlemen, the time has now come, when the true conservative men of all parties should unite for the sake of the Union. I propose, sir—"THE UNION: We will stand by *all* who stand by *it*."

Mr. SPENCER being called on for a sentiment, rose and said:

Mr. PRESIDENT: We have assembled to do honor to a distinguished guest from the East, for the service he has rendered his country in the recent struggle through which it has passed. I am certain, sir, it will afford him pleasure to see upon the record of this day's proceedings, the name of another statesman, who has immortalized himself in the same contest to preserve the Union, one who comes from another quarter, the South. In view of what he has done, of the part he has borne, in saving this happy country from the awful consequences of disunion, I am unwilling that this meeting should dissolve without giving him a place in our proceedings, and transmitting his name to posterity in the record we are now preparing. All who have been in any way connected with that great event are entitled to the outpourings of our hearts, and should ever be remembered with smiles of admiration. Instead of being engaged in an unholy crusade against the Constitution, all their energies have been directed to the preservation of a government reared by our revolutionary sires, cemented by their blood, and under which we have all lived with unbounded prosperity and unequalled happiness. Our ancestors struggled to relieve themselves from the shackles of tyranny. They entered into a contest for the rights of the people, and to redeem them from oppression. They fought for liberty. It was then,

"Fair freedom, bursting from the realms of day,
Poured forth, indignant, her prophetic lay.
Oppressors listened to her with dismay;
The inspiring notes, thro' air quick winged their way,
And sounding to old ocean's utmost shore,
Bade freedom's sons arise, and slavery be no more."

The event fills the mind with scenes, patriotic, grand, and sublime. Their heroic valor achieved our independence, and the result was our glorious Union; the proud fabric of human wisdom, unrivalled and unequalled.

To perpetuate that Union, where liberty, virtue, genius, and science dwell, "the asylum of all men," the ark of safety to every wanderer, amidst the tumultuous elements of this world's politics—the ardent exertions and untiring devotion of our guest, and those associated with him in the contest, have been given, and with patriotism unsurpassed. By their exertions, the glory of the nation remains undivided. The chivalry of the Navy and the gallantry of the Army are still national. They are untarnished, and still shine in undimmed splendor in the American firmament. Not one star has been stricken from our national flag, nor has our proud bird, the emblem of our nation's glory, lost one feather from his beautiful plumage.

Sir, of all the men who have earned for themselves an immortal fame in the bitter strife, which we have with such deep distress witnessed in the attempt to overthrow our Government, none have distinguished themselves more than the honorable H. S. Foote, of Mississippi. [Great applause.] The fanaticism of the North, had, by its unfeeling policy, produced a flame in the South which required the keenest sagacity of a statesman to arrest. A flame which, if not arrested, and that speedily, would necessarily consume all devotion to the Union. In such a crisis, when so much feeling was involved, in consequence of the mad attacks which were constantly being made upon the domestic institutions of the South, the tendency of which was to drench their fields with blood, to desolate their homes, and desecrate their household gods, the question arose, how was such a crisis to be met? Men of the purest virtue and well-tried patriotism, called for a Southern Convention, to consider the question of dissolution.

The mind shudders at a crisis, so awful, as to drive honest men to the contemplation of an extreme, overwhelming to all the glory of the past and the grandeur of the future. In such a crisis, though opposed by some of his best and warmest friends, though denounced at home as opposing the interest and wishes and happiness of his constituents, Mr. Foote, looking to the Union as our best ark of safety, and relying upon the strength of the Government as the best possible security to arrest the suicidal arm of the abolitionist, and of all and any disloyalist who resists the guarantees of the Constitution, came to the rescue with his brilliant talents and indomitable courage. Well may he exclaim,

Exegi monumentum ære perennius.

In conclusion, I offer the following sentiment:

Hon. H. S. Foote: A man made for the times, who, rising above the storms of passion, devoted himself, soul and body, his commanding eloquence and undaunted spirit, to the perpetuation of our happy Union, entire and undivided. [Drank standing and with enthusiastic applause.]

The following toast was proposed by G. C. MORGAN, esq., of St. Mary's county:

The judiciary of Maryland—whatever difference of opinion may be entertained as to its organization, the value of its administration is appreciated, and its purity is without stain or reproach. [Great applause.]

Judge CHAMBERS said, in replying to the above sentiment, that to be called upon, in this presence, at this hour, after what we have heard, was of all things the least expected by him, certainly the least desired.

What had been said was surely enough to fill the measure of one day's glory. He would, however, ask attention, while he noticed one remark which had fallen from our distinguished guest. It was that "his mission had been to sustain the Constitution and the Union."

Judge C. believed, as firmly as he believed any fact in history, that such was the case. The same superintending Providence that had guarded and guided the patriots of the Revolution, that had controlled and directed our destinies, and made us a great nation, that same invisible but omniscient Being that had raised up a Washington to lead our armies and to establish the Union, had also raised up a Webster to defend and sustain it. Yes, sir, that was and is his "mission." And most faithfully has he so far fulfilled his vocation. Ages to come will testify to this truth. It had been the prominent work of his whole public, useful life. Sir, said Judge C., it was long since, my delight to hear this noble specimen of an American Senator, utter, to an admiring world, profound lessons of constitutional law, and patriotic sentiments of deep devotion to the Union. Never has a crisis occurred, when, amid the warring elements of the political storm, his voice has not been heard; and where Webster stood, there was the rallying point for the friends of the Union and the Constitution.

He has told us that Washington, when in this city he surrendered his sword, and said he had finished the work assigned him, was not aware that the duty assigned him extended to the latest time.

Sir, he is perhaps the only man who does not perceive that the same remark applies with equal force to himself. His "mission" is to posterities yet to people the wide surface of this American world; yes, sir, to all people and nations of the earth. The lessons of patriotism and political wisdom, so eloquently and fervently taught in his speeches, his writings, and his life, will be text books for all who are to succeed us.

Sir, that Providence, whose high behests he has obeyed, will cause his memory to be embalmed for all time in the hearts of his countrymen. Generations, yet unborn, will rise up and pay the tribute of thankful praise to the memory of him, to whose efforts they are so largely indebted for the unparalleled extent of their civil, political, and religious blessings.

And now, Mr. President, a word or two as to matters nearer our own time and condition. I have long been a listener to discussions about the Constitution. For the last four or five months we have all heard, in constant association with another idea, that of "Reform," "Constitutional Reform."

Now, sir, I am quite aware of the place where I stand, of the presence in which I speak, of the multitude and variety of opinions here entertained about this said matter of "Constitutional Reform." It is, indeed, a very narrow plank on which I must walk, for no body in this pleasant circle of harmonious friends must be offended or disturbed. Yet, sir, I will venture, will hazard a suggestion, will just intimate one particular, in which, it may be, we may all unite, in despite of our various notions on many others. I offer it in the shape of the following sentiment:

"Reform—the most thorough "Constitutional Reform"—to every man, who does not himself love, and teach his children and his children's children to love, the Union, as the first duty of an American.

The following toast was proposed by J. W. CRISFIELD, ESQ.:

"The Chancellor of Maryland: the enlightened jurist and statesman; he has honored his State by his devotion to her service."

Chancellor JOHNSON responded to the toast, substantially in the following terms:

It is certainly very gratifying to me, Mr. President, that upon an occasion like the present, any poor service which I may have rendered the State, in any capacity, should be deemed worthy of remembrance.

We have assembled this evening to do honor to one of the most distinguished statesmen of the country, and to be permitted to be here, and to unite in this tribute of gratitude for his patriotic devotion to her welfare, is of itself a privilege, of which any citizen may well be proud.

Upon many former occasions the eminent man, whose eloquent voice we have just listened to with delight, had poured out the abundant treasures of his great intellect, in expounding the Constitution of his country, and vindicating the cause of human liberty. In no age, nor in any country, had more eloquent or powerful appeals in behalf of free institutions been made, than had fallen from his lips; but upon all such occasions, prior to the part he took in the discussion of the questions, which, during the first session of the recent Congress, so violently convulsed the country, he was cheered on and sustained by the known approbation of those whose immediate representative he was. He could not but have anticipated their entire approval of his sentiments; and the beautiful thoughts, and eloquent language in which they were clothed, he well knew, would be treasured in their hearts.

When, however, he rose in the Senate, on the 7th of March, 1850, to express his views upon the questions to which I have referred, he occupied a position totally unlike any in which theretofore he had been placed.

The country had waited with anxiety, but without distrust, to hear the voice of the foremost statesman of the North. The questions under consideration had engaged the exclusive attention of the Senate for months; they had been debated with a vehemence and intensity of feeling, without parallel in our previous history; and the elements of discord, from one extremity of the Union to the other, seemed to have usurped and beaten down the calm counsels of judgment and reason.

No approach seemed then to have been made towards the adjustment of the controversy, and the hearts of the lovers of peace and tranquility were filled with dismay.

It was under these untoward circumstances that the Senator from Massachusetts rose to address the Senate and the country, and appealed to them in tones of earnest entreaty to "hear him for his cause."

Now had arrived the time, if it had never come before, to try if he was "current coin indeed." It was known, none knew better than he, that in pleading the cause of the Union and the Constitution, he would expose himself to the obloquy of a portion of his contituents; and that the sentiments he was about to express upon some of the great questions of the day, would place him in opposition to the current of public opinion in his State.

But these considerations were, as all, who well knew Mr. Webster, knew they would be, totally ineffectual to deter him from throwing the weight of his great name, and the influence of his powerful intellect, in the scale of peace upon that side, upon the success of which depended the tranquility of the country, if not the preservation of the Union itself. And, when, dashing from him every consideration connected with local interests or sectional prejudices, he plead for peace, harmony, and union; and in tones of thrilling eloquence, and with arguments of controlling power, he prostrated and overwhelmed the fanatics on the one hand, and the impracticables on the other, he seemed to realize the poet's dream, and to exhibit that rare creation:

"Where every god did seem to set his seal, to give the world assurance of a man."

But, Mr. President, while remembering with grateful hearts the services of our distinguished guest, it does not become us to overlook, or to be silent, with regard to the patriotic statesmen who joined their efforts to his, in rescuing their country from the danger then impending over it; and in this connexion permit me to say, and I say it with a sincerity fully commensurate with my sense of the merits of the distinguished gentleman, whose name I am about to mention, that I consider every friend of freedom, and free institutions of government, throughout the world, deeply indebted to General Cass for the part he took upon the trying occasion to which we have been referring.

He, too, came from a section of the country in which opinions adverse to a just and amicable settlement of the disturbing questions prevailed to a considerable extent. Indeed, at one time, he stood fettered by legislative instructions to pursue a course in opposition to his own patriotic instincts. But, shaking himself free from these, he nobly proclaimed, that rather than give a vote which his conscience condemned, he would at the proper time resign the high trust which his State had conferred upon him, and retire to private life. For this patriotic resolution, which unquestionably would have been fulfilled, and for the powerful and effectual aid which he rendered to the great cause, of restoring the peace of the country, and the preservation of the Republic, he has won for himself, and will receive, its undying gratitude.

I am also quite sure, Mr. President, that the name of General FOOTE is heard by this company with emotions of unqualified pleasure. None among the friends of the series of measures, which we may well hope have or will restore quiet to a distracted people, were more earnest, more efficient, or more resolute than he. Like the eminent men whose names have been mentioned, he likewise exposed himself to dangers at home, the result of local prejudices, from which, natures less determined and self-sacrificing than his, might have shrunk with dismay.

But, with a courage which no perils could damp, an impetuous ardor and love of country, in comparison with which all considerations of mere personal advantage were but as dust in the balance, he was, at every hazard, found among the foremost of those who were contending for the welfare of the whole nation. Eloquent and chivalric by nature, of warm temperament and resistless energy, he has already placed himself high in the public regard, and associated his name with the leading men of the Republic.

There is another name, Mr. President, which will recur to all, when the citizens of this country meet to do honor to its great benefactors, the name of HENRY CLAY. It rings in the ear like the spirit-stirring tones of the trumpet, and never will be forgotten until every feeling of gratitude, and all appreciation of high desert, is extirpated from the human breast.

When, during his day, did the bugle sound the charge, or the sentinel proclaim the alarm, that HENRY CLAY was not ready to lead the charge, or defend the beleaguered battlements of the Republic against all assailants?

Thirty years before, when this same question of African slavery spread itself in darkening shadows over our political firmament, the great Statesman of Kentucky beat back the raging billows of discord, and dispersed the threatening cloud; and now again, when age has blanched his hair and somewhat bent his majestic form, and quenched his fiery glance, we find him once more in the Senate, in the front rank, if not the foremost, of the defenders of the nation against the dangers which this institution, so vital to the South, never fails to create when brought under discussion. It may, Mr. President, with truth be said, that whenever danger has menaced his country, during the long period of Mr. CLAY's life, he has been looked to as one of her chief protectors; and I am sure I speak the sentiment of the whole people, when I express the earnest hope that he may be long spared to enjoy their gratitude and contribute to their welfare.

Mr. President, I ask permission, before I take my seat, to introduce another name to this company, I refer to the honorable Mr. DICKINSON, late Senator from New York, as a gentleman eminently worthy to be remembered upon occasions like the present. In the late great crisis through which the country has passed, he displayed abilities, firmness, and patriotism; and Whig though I am, and he has always been a prominent member of the other great political party, if I had held a seat in the Legislature of New York when a Senator was recently elected, and there had been the slightest ground for suspecting that the Whig candidate for that high post was not perfectly orthodox upon the questions upon which, in my judgment, the integrity of the Constitution and the safety of the Union depend, as I live and breathe, I would have voted for Mr. DICKINSON. He had been tried, thoroughly tested, and found to be composed of sterling metal, without dross or impurity; and I should have been proud to have shown my sense of his high merits, by trampling party considerations beneath my feet, and voting for him, when those considerations conflicted in the slightest degree with others, before which they dwindle into insignificance.

The "higher law" doctrine found no approval with him. That doctrine, by which a man, living under an organized government, enjoying the benefit of its laws, and protected by its authority, may set up a standard in his own breast, by which the validity of other laws, not quite to his taste, may be tried.

Mr. President, years may pass, and I sincerely hope many may pass, before the country will be called upon to undergo another ordeal so severe as that through which we have recently gone. But, though the trial was a hard one, and the bonds of the Union were fearfully strained, they held us together; and may we not trust that, if a strand was broken or overstrained, it will be replaced with a new one; and that additional cords will be found which neither rust or violence will break?

If, however, this should not be so; if this glorious Union is destined to be dissolved; if fate has so decreed, and the government and temple built by Washington and his compeers, and dedicated to human liberty, shall fall; if our venerable Constitution, and the Union, of which it is the life's blood, though defended by WEBSTER, and the great patriots and statesmen of the land, must perish at last, and no human agency is capable of averting the doom, still his and their names will be remembered, and repeated as examples worthy to be imitated by those who may, in future times, contend for the rights of man. Mr. President, I offer this sentiment:

"OUR DISTINGUISHED GUEST.—When his calumniators shall have been forgotten, he will be remembered as the great constitutional lawyer of his day; unsurpassed in his advocacy of Republican Institutions, and of the union of these States."

MR. JENIFER said he would have made a few remarks had not the learned Chancellor of Maryland "stolen his thunder;" but, as he despaired of a reclamation by a bill in equity, he cordially approved the elegant eulogy passed upon the distinguished son of New York, whose efforts in support of the Union, when shaken to its centre, are found on the side of his country. Mr. J. said he would offer the following sentiment:

DANIEL S. DICKINSON—a statesman of the old Roman school—a willing sacrifice for his country's good.

Mr. WEBSTER being about to retire, the Hon. WM. COST JOHNSON rose, and addressed the company as follows:

Mr. PRESIDENT: I shall not tax you, nor this distinguished assemblage, but for a moment; and in that moment, to offer a sentiment of my own heart, which sentiment, I am sure, abides in every bosom around me, to one whose life, from youth, has been dedicated to teaching the purest morals and the most exalted patriotism, whose highest ambition has been to see this glorious nation advance in prosperity and honorable renown; and whose wonderful efforts of light and life will pass to other ages, and be read, side by side, with Cicero and Tacitus. I propose the health, the prosperity, the long life of DANIEL WEBSTER.

The company drank this toast with many cheers. Mr. WEBSTER responded in a most happy manner to the remarks of Mr. JOHNSON, and retired from the company.

www.ingramcontent.com/pod-product-compliance
Lightning Source LLC
LaVergne TN
LVHW011145110826
845150LV00008B/2513
9781418192532